Dark Energy

BY DANIEL WILCOX

Published by
Diminuendo Press
Imprint of Cyberwizard Productions
1205 N. Saginaw Boulevard #D
PMB 224
Saginaw, Texas 76179

ISBN: 978-1-936021-11-6
Library of Congress Control Number: 2009930918

First Edition:

Table of Contents

To Donald and Elma Wilcox
A father and mother who gave me a rich childhood and encouraged
my creativity

Dark Energy

Featureless dark energy
From vacuum fluctuations
Of the quantum metatech
Pervade the hidden universe
Permeating all of space timed
Expanding outward
Creating the exploding cosmos
Accelerating beyond
The Scalar field or cosmological constant
Strong negative pressure, yes, creative tension
And the brightness of the supernova
Crossing billions of light years--redshifted
Evidence of spaced darkness
Oh Quintessence--superstringed vibrations
From the Musician of all Light
Only the Eternal One
Can make and hide it
Among the galaxies and stars
For us to stare up into the visible darkness
Spangled with Light

After the Loss

all my nerves torn loose
in the streets dancing jangles
staccatoed electric wires
ripped loose from my telephone
souled dangerous lightning night

Published in MadSwirl

The Wedding

laughter, rowdy noise
in a rollicking hall of revelers
partying
at a crowded table
of night wedding,
our parted
separating

The Art of Rebounding

A basketball and hoop of game
Is played by the lanky guy linked
To seeing himself smaller than
The shorter opponent, who man
To man out jumps his taller
And swishes the ball through the net
Leaving the tall player caught,
Rebounded to his shortness.

West Yellowstone

Now its all rather vague,
        how on a windy summer midnight

I was on the leg
        up highway 191 far from daylight,

The sky blacked and blued
        above me, my legs groaned in pain,

And stranded on this parked avenue
        I didn't want to sleep in the rain.

Rounding a bend in the road
        I came upon a guy who gave me a ride

Though he had a truck load
        and let me off in the town business side.

Drunks were roaming around;
        Yet I found the gazebo alone,

So I thankfully bedded down
        in the city park of West Yellowstone,

        And all so strange,
                I had no reservation arranged.

A Miner's Bullion

with charcoal hair
        shifting down
                to round shoulders,
        shading precious metal
                of staring copper face;

earth's expression from
        iron ore tinged lips and tongue;

scarlet mark on neck of bronzed smoothness,
                silver-blossed body,
golden thighs are not cross
        down to large feet
                sticky wet with Yellowstone watery brine
and sand
--east of Butte
        Montana shimmering west

Published by Full of Crow

News Item: The Dentists

Cavity deep in the Egyptian sand
Sleuthed near an old step pyramid,
Grave robbers tool about for dead gold,
The tomb of the dentists is found--
Pictographed and mummified
Bodies under moldering mud brick,
But the thieves get caught by the police,
And the site crowds, filled by arc-finders
Reveling in the discovery of dead lives,
Of those who strove to counter decay
But couldn't fill the 'whole' loss of death--
Deep in the tunnels of premature burial;
So true of us all, dying anytime soon.

My half-opened fish sandwich
Minus a hefty bite, I swallow and
Leave the busy Golden Arches, ambling
 My way down the bright Canadian street.

Blaring new motel neons dim out the stars,
And SUV's, with mostly BC plates, line a Comfort Inn
Up from some Quality place here in Kamloops,
An expanding tourist zoo with a far western angle.
I wonder why in the vast outdoors so West
I've seen no wildlife on the long upward drive,
Except that small squirrel below Seattle.
But then I am suddenly interrupted--
As a large black bulk of night lobs
Into the empty concrete of street,
No circus crowd to be pleased.

The dark blob of bear glances my way;
I stop alive in my fast food tracks,
My fried fish like some jumping
Northern salmon half way to my mouth,
Wafting out sauce in the cool night breeze;
But the large bear ignores my late supper
And lopes into the crowded parking lot
Of the Comfort Inn, past a PT Cruiser
And a staid green Ford Mustang,
Maybe headed for the trash dumpster
And a late evening garbage binge.

I hurry for cover, yelling quickly
To an ignorant woman walking her Chihuahua.
She avidly pushes buttons for, I guess,
The Royal Mounted Bear Keepers.

The Wheel

within the circle of the wheel
from the rim steel spoke
of each other spoke
how inferiorly shafted
but the hub laughed and laughed

You Wish A Letter

what is there to say

    i can't lay on the sidewalk
            gazing up at your eyes
like in the month after may

what is there to do
    i can't touch you with my hands
            caressing your face and your feet
like i wanted to in june

what shall i say
    i will convey my feelings
            writing to you on this paper
like in the month after may

what shall i do
    i will love you with my words
            touching your heart and your mind
like i wanted to in june

The Volcano

liquid lead
rising from
the insurmountable
    depths
     of
     the
    chasm
     earth;
the sea a molten mass.
            the sun a marble balloon
buoyed in the oceaned fog
          then
      descending into nothingness

Body Language

The constant elbow lady,
Loud and boisterous
At our feasted table,
Dominates the airwaves
South of the polished bar

Where the silent and calm
Bar Lass-tender works alone
Short, stilled, and observant,
Her arms lowered aside
Employed to attend patrons
Not there, but here

Where the elbowed breath
0f our table lady is close enough
To inhale, whose moved arms
Keep poking us two drinkers
Next to her as she loudly laughs,
Jutting her elbows about like batons
And guffaws with her many
Bodied words.

The Kindly Llama

There once was a man named Osama
Who humans claimed the terror's puma,
But then Bush shouted, Cease!
Don't be a mean wild beast;
Instead be a kind Dalai Lama.

Surreal Morning

bulky morro rock
floats heavy on the narrow gray
ocean fog strata, sedimentary air
while the ocean's soapy crashing
churns combustible froth
and advances up the shore sand
the sun orange
in the fogged foam below
the floating ghost ship

Published in Erbacce

Aging

 Lost goals
Superficial routines—rigmarole
I throw lifelines out
They flunk down but skitter back
Empty
Treading time

Art Clasps

A Monet moment
            splashes in vibrancy--
                        yellowish-orange irises
                                    rise from
blue and green

                                    130 years after the

paint.

Below the beauty

But the impractical clasping
                        of the momentary irises
                                    by impressed
paintbrush strokes

Hold
        scintillating eye glances
                        and shimmering lights up for
us to see,

                        saved from
                                    the oblivion of another
time and place.

Likewise a fellow traveler, I clasp words

                        to this sheet, my own flat canvas--
irised memories

For new eyes
            down
            through
            future
            landscaped
            time.
First *published in the Mississippi Crow Magazine*

Up Early

In the gray-hazed dawn
Pale light blossoms
Softly explode from a violet tree
Rising by a jade-green hedge
Birdsong morning

Published in the Mississippi Crow Magazine

Montana's History Lesson

Bulky Pompei's Pillar
Towers over the Yellowstone Rivering,
A rugged brown bluff
Engraved with historic graffiti
With Clark's signatured
Declaration still writ large
Behind Plexiglas for us to gawk,
But Lewis ended it all;
Still the icy water courses on
Toward the Big Muddy
Finally down to the Gulf,
Each of us a brief tag
In this
Muddled flow of time.

Published in Lunarosity

Cold as Hell

We stood in the sub zero
Montana ranch pasture,
Below the gauntlet of a gray sky,

Five cow hands leaning forward,
Our boots deep in the brown
Stubble and crusted snow.

We stepped closer, crunching
Ice, but mute, breathing
Fog, our hands still and numb,

To watch this high noon rancher
In the Levi jacket and tan hat,
His ears red and fingers blooded.

Oblivious to the minus degrees,
He semi-crouched and tugged,
Pulling at a panting half-born calf;

Her head and neck out, but stuck
In the womb of this bloated cow,
Agonizing in the bloody snow.

Thrashing, undelivered,
The brown mother bellowed
But all I remember--the cold.

Published in The Externalist and in Frostwriting

Sierra Hiker

Golden trails, loving strands
I follow with my eyes;

Radiant smile, glowing face
Lighting away my shadows;

Diligent hands, plying fingers
Latticing strewn moments into art;

Fruitful tree, slender body
Open to me, enclosed to us;

Caring heart, giving spirit
Surprising gifts daily to me.

Court Hearing

Spacious, vast room in cedar
High and lifted up the judge's platform
With the California Seal above

Below, the wing-shaped table
In obeisance at the foot of order
With boom black mikes rising up
To the 5 formal persons sitting down
Submitted, respectful
Silent, waiting to speak

The white-haired, black-robed
Judge flips and scans Rod's awards
Fancy sheets of 'principal,' honor, attendance
Straight A's festooning the formal records

Then staring down at Rod, he asks informally,
Why are you here?

Rod peers passive

And the parents puzzle the jigsaw
Of their son
And the missing
Parts

Published in Right Hand Pointing

Yosemite

And when I feel crippled in my mind

    I remember that young man on the turn out
                          by the asphalt--
                          down
                          the granite canyon
   boulders strewn in the gnashing river—where he sat,
cradled
                          in his chromed wheel
chair,
                          stubby haired, thumb
extending
                          his face a calm question

                          to the window glass
stares
                                    of
touring cars.

Published in The Indite Circle

The Miser

His wife relaxes the evened hours
With a solitaire hand,
Their children squander eyed time
Gaming into the midnight

But he worries every minute's less,
Squeezing out drabbed work-points
From the tube of life, pinched flat;

Frugal elder of the clock,
He pockets
The moment,
Hoards the seconds,
Ever goes for thirds;

In the locked vault
Of his work,
No coinage of pleasure
Only
Collecting
Paper
With
A will.

Published by Word Catalyst Magazine

Playing Heir Ball

Our historic cat coughed up
a wadded brown object,
thumb-sized
and yarned…

Ah forget
The long-winding 'tail';
go pell-mell
to your cultural
memory--
what was
your latest
cough up?

Published in The Clockwise Cat

Harvest Time

burned-over dreams in the rusted oil drum
behind the white house of fallen child
midwest blown by the thundered storm

hedged branches, clumped together nearby
waiting to become ashes wafted cumulus
piles of browned cuttings lost to history

yet writing stems up greening between
the cracks in the disjointed concrete walk
behind the parsonage, weeds of wonder
between the slabs of the displaced past

in front raking my fallen memories up
shoving those windblown scatterings
off the green lawn dumping them over
down into the drainage-ditched pile

rising up, 3 feet of dry-colored splash
a crinkly mass of discarded leaving
bursting red, yellow, orange, and tan
for struggling kids-of-heart to jump in

Published in Words-Myth

Two salesmen
Fight at the registered counter
Over inventoried accuracy
And the improper return of a buzz saw;
The younger suddenly strikes
With pit-vipered words,
The fanged-mouth of the occasion
Sharking his parting teeth,
"This is why I sleep warm
While you sleep alone."
The swim of conversation
Wrecks on one's jagged ambition,
The dark fin of daggered end,
A slippery bottom
Of hidden deep
Drowning
One.

Published in The Poetry Warrior

Walking the Night

saplings blacken along
the sidewalk against the misted night,
a refracted light sky over
wrought iron candelabras on stands
lamping the coasted evening

Published by Writer's Ink

After the Yellow Warning Light

At the stop before the exit
I hunch, feathered, on my late day perch
Above the overhead red light
Next to the enameled quick cam,
Black next to white,
Glance at the camera
Then down the lens
Wide the aperture
To the hurrying busy cars
Gazing down through time
To the future deaths
Of the preoccupants,
Of so many,
So it goes
Evermore.

Fall Impression

In that fall of Nebraska's weather so dying,
Sun-jaded trees ungreened and thundered color

Reverberating the world, 'Going' to the limit;
They left tremoring rainbows earth-bound and shingled

In the wind--melted yellow, orange, and maroon,
Fingerpaints amess, leaved in the black wrought branches;

Then with the stroke of the northerly gusts,
The zagged etchings counterwheeled in swirling emotion—

Hacking our senses, hueing our minds until glazed--
And so reeled diagonally down in that kaleidoscoping
Monet.

Published in The Write Side Up

Rock Life

White-capped wind roars around
Huge volcanic buttes swimming north
Off the Oregon Coast
Like asymmetrical gray whales
Leaving splashing trails of white water
Behind in the slate green ocean
Yes, waves churning around
The behemoths, frothing

Published in The Houston Literary Review

The Shell Zebra Mussels In
Neither white nor black,
Confusingly mixed the bivale zebra,
A tiny hitchhiker of water ways,
'Mussels' in on our lived-in boats
Encrusting us in a hanger's attack,
Striped micro-wolves in shelled fleece,
Cultural mussels of nescient devilment,
Molochian mollusks, voracious,
Yet with a deceiving lustrous lining;

They invade our lake of life
Innocent-looking,
Dark elongated hard 'sells'
With no reservoir-ations, who
Attach themselves to us voyagers
And clog our inners with their
Smelly shell remains,
Foul our abodes
Obstruct and damage
Human communion;

Clean your inner 'bilge'
Of these muscling-in
Devourers, small-time
Inn wreckers.

*Recent News: The California Department of Fish and Game uses 24
mussel-sniffing dogs for the sole purpose of discovering zebra mussels
on boats. Boats longer than 24 feet will be quarantined for 14 days.*

Published in Word Catalyst Magazine

Under the sky world
Below the sloshing white caps,
Liquid life undulates down through
The watery sphere's domain;

A soft brilliance of rays from
Above strike silver lines down
Through the deepening green
While strange denizens move in
Rhythmic concertos;

A great turtle flippers alone, dull-jade submarine;
Then sheened orchestras of under creatures
Tuna, halibut, and cod their way
In a Strauss waltz west with the current;

Snorkeling deeper
Finned life multiplics to the seventh
Wide oceans crowded round,
Translucent, entrailed, scaled and numinous;
Scuttling down to endless flips of tail
Iridescent, orange, purple, yellow;

Suddenly spades-black ink billows out
Deep in the guts of the world's water
To the side of the neon coral,
So mused reefs,
Expanding, darkening the undermost
Arms, arms, arms, and arms—
Many a league,
The fabled
One.

Published in The Greensilk Journal

Pomona Hills

Reptile scales,
                clouds of snake skin
            withering
                across the lair of smog
        and the magnesium sun
                        over the auburn shekeled hills;
                            grain waves of wheat
                                    in the boiler
wind
            -yes,
                    red combines at the
edge of fields.

Published in Identity Theory

Under the Big Sky

Half a dozen years clouded back,
        looking for three missing calves,
Rough and thunder day, my rawhide of memory,
        under the big sky near Bozeman;

But now under the metal-blazed Middle Eastern sun
        I disc the rock strewn objected earth
Dragging this 'branding iron,'
        rivening rows of baked earth, blading
The hills southeast of Nazareth,
        leaving a sky trail of smoked dust
To swirl high over the Jordan River
        hazing up the murderous sky--

        one kibbutznik

Published in Word Catalyst Magazine

Her face white-puffed and plastic
Rouged and lipped carmine
Couched in the satin pillow;
Why am I staring down
At this female all dressed out?
I don't know this woman!

The shock richters all deep
To my marrow and mien;
This is a mannequined second
Not my dear aunt in her final end.
Almost smiling in consternation,
I wake up at this funeral!

My deepened sorrow lightens,
But I force myself to tradition
And stare down in meditation
At this stiff of skin and bones,
The body, a perfect figure
Of modern funeraled artifice--
I don't know this woman!

Where's her so scrawny face
Wrinkled to prune and 50ish glasses,
Her ornery wiles and devious ways?
Stray mutts played in her bathtub
(The same size as this metal coffin)
Their residue smelling her house
While she placed pet ads in the news
Making loads of money on free dogs.
Where have her shenanigans gone?
I wake up at this funeral!

Even if this rigid corpse had been
Modeled close to her formal picture--
That hangs like a small billboard

For the traffic of the bereaved--
I know this would not be her
Lying still and so stiffly proper;
Not my aunt who used to walk
Down main street, her black
Spider monkey throned on her shoulder
Slurping an ice cream cone.
I don't know this woman!

She would have displayed bananas
And stuffed monkeys in her casket
Or two of her real apes who used
Gallivant around in Huggies
And bring iced Cokes from the frig
To her skinny, bed-ridden self.
I don't know this woman!

I sigh in lively relief and stroll
Buoyantly back to the rear
Of the viewing room away
From this 3,000 dollar joke
Glad that the deadweight
Of her emphysema-ness
Has been cut clean away.
We wake up at this funeral!

The certain pruning cuts us deep
To the 'morrow,' we who remain
But I do know, really, that my dear aunt
Is not here in this still, prim cadaver
Thank God! We awake!

Published in Lunarosity

wind 'gutles' the animal sound in the trees
outside
moon and sharp stars strike no more
visible
inside the bunkhouse, boots lean and a bed
unmade
upon it, old blankets and a 'mutted' dog
curled
up brim of a soiled hat hangs above not
gone
their calloused master drove away
after
unsaddling his shivered horse in the barn
left
in the snowy dark without his whining dog
alone
it is gut shot by the grinning boss at
noon
in the moonless day
below
the animal sounds in the
trees

Published in The Driftwood Review

Getting the Slip

Another
Editor's slip
Pulled success
Out from under me--
But since scientists
Say over 50% of our
Genes inhabit bananas—
I must be the human
Peeling out
--As I slip--
Laughter Pealing,
Tolling time;
Foraging
In my roots, branching out,
Redwooded though fired,
Bristleconedness
Up growing above
Rejections littering
Underneath--
So much compost.

Published in Mississippi Crow Magazine

Wasted Wealth

His plum-stained hands,
He washes thoroughly at the sink
But still feels the hot flesh
Of the blood-red fruit that
Plummeted the ground
In their backyard, wasted wealth
He plopped into plastic bags full
And finally dumped about seven
Into the stained trash can
Where the crimson spheres will oven
In the hot afternoon sun
And dry to pruned excess;
His strange plum tree so like himself,
A redneck worker
Bringing forth abundance
Only to drop
His all onto the dark bar floor
On another three-night bender.

Published in Oak Bend Review

Facing the Storm

Out beyond the sea wall
At the far end of the long tar-black pier
Jutting into the raging torrent,
Many still lean into the rampaging wind
Up against the worn guard rail,
Gazing out to the swirling turbulence;
Assaulted by the acrid fish pier smell
And the mackerel guts
Spewed on the dock's warped boards;

But Neil turns
Leaving the wanton churn, and walks
Half a block to the mariners' chapel
Its flipper-like shingles worn and damp,
But inside all polished wood and
Decked with banners of shimmering light;

He bows and 'kneels' at the altar,
While Jasmine aglow, adorned
In her white crystalline dress
Waltzes over to him.
They embrace and rise
To counter the coming storm.

Black Light

My eyes pressed and I slipt
    in under her fleece cloth
    in the desire of my mind.

Her eyes were iridescent
    in the blackness of herself
    in the darkness of the house.

She spoke a southern accent
    from carved ebony lips
    from a northern white city.

I spoke with unprejudiced hint
    from separate loneliness
    from a dusky existence.

I wished to be able to protect
    against the loss of innocence
    against our blotted culture.

She was black light intent
    against the vulgar glare of war
    against the shadowy white.

Published in The Recusant

Growing up on the plains of Nebraska
Far below Canada's fertile dominion,
What I first knew of you way up yonder
(If you get the drift) was deeply sensed,
The polar bearness of your blistery winters
Blizzarding down icy cold white over us,
 Leaving snow higher than I to shovel.

And while I sledded down Terrill's hill
I never snowshoed, ice fished, or played hockey
But did move to 'skyed' Montana where a Cheyenne
(Not shy) maiden gave me a red hickey
Next to the silver Reservation water tower
Only a cool night's drive from your Alberta,
Which I never met though both are under the stars

Until I fished in the lucid Boundary Waters
And once wandered by boat into lakeful Ontario
Because we couldn't see the lined border in the
Sky blue waters but only the many rainbow trout
Who swam around my dangling bait 20 feet down
Refusing to bite, evidently not liking an alien;
We turned back before the Coast Guard came.

So call me deprived, so unCanadian
Well, that's not quite true. I did see you on TV—
Dudley Do-right and the Royal Mounties
And read dog sled "tales" forested in the snow banks

Of your goodly country so vast and richly cold.
So how is it that I have traveled the world
Half way round but never snowshoed north to visit?

Published in The Centrifugal Eye

Discarding

On the way to the town dump
The junk in the back jostles in the turn.
Dark blue clouds curtain rain down.

I pull onto the miry dirt road
Past the leaning one-story screens
Where dark birds and wrens perch

But launch to flight as I pass and reverse.
Backing up the Sienna to the trash heap
I get out and step in the hogged mud,

Throw out the old bed banisters
A rusted bike, worn shirts and 'genes,'
All my grouchy frustration;

Yes and my enlarged head tilted
With church dogma, loads of heavy fact,
And too many years of clouded regret.

Driving home—so empty and satisfied.

Published in Tipton Poetry Journal

Shadowed Garden

in the long backlawn
ansel-adam shadows
grow in the late afternoon
extending across the grass,
shading the steel dog dish,
the hula hoop, and the wagon--
a one-dimensional garden
slowly tended by the leaving sun,
only to be hoed under by the dusk

Published in The Green Silk Journal

In the far lane
DIVORCES
BANKRUPTCIES
Blare out west
Tall scarlet letters
Blocked and bold
From the slam side
Of the grim van with
Abandon--
This advertised
Low reaper
Of life's road path
Doesn't do
Plain death.

Published in The Scruffy Dog Review

Gargoyle

Feeling listless
Lestful, full-less?
Gargoyle your soul's
Virused mouth
Washing away the
Frightful germs of
Lusterine horror from
Your throated spirit,
Out of their deceitful lair;
Purge the demoned den
Of your snakeful brain,
Then spit clean.

Published in The Clockwise Cat

Research Filing Cabinets

The pages of history torn loose and filed
In manila folders away in the grey cabinet,

Letters' ink still darkening my busy fingers
Of too many newspaper yesterdays;

Printed faces in strident or friendly poses,
Even curvaceous bodies that now slowly molder

Under the bright sheen of deep metal caskets
Yesterday's news-dirt buried behind steel,

While their data and dotted images hang
There incased in immaculate office rooms

Waiting for the hand of future's need,
Living a virtual afterlife.

Published in Mad Swirl

Aesopian Snail

Dashing his slow bodied trail
The white snail on the gray cement
Scoots clock-hand down
The sloping driveway;
I stoop to pick up the newspaper
Unwrap headlines to
13 soldiers killed by insurgents;
I walk back reading--
Crunch.

Published in The Cerebral Catalyst

'Utter' Common Sense

Have ya' been suckin'
At modern science's teat?

Com 'on! it's normal sense,
Visual at least--the earth's flat.

If we were roundly twirlin',
We'd fall wide or down at least.

Just look about—do you feel
You're standin' angled?

What duggin' nonsense,
What dream-stuff is this?

How are we walkin' sideways
On a huge spinnin' ball?

Haven't ya ever heard of
The four corners of the earth?

What happens to the wild west
If we drive and arrive at east?

And as for humans comin'
From an ancient prime-mate,

Silliness indeed; my wife
Doesn't monkey around,

Not even in my dreams;
Cow down on that!

Published in The Clockwise Cat

First Day Writing

The pensive silence,
Glaring window glass,
And eyed 'pupils' filled
With blocked wander.

The pause of clocking
Hands and a smudge
Writ large on the desk's
Blank, shiny surface.

From outside the class
Comes the clunk-drop
Of a heavy metal bin
By the trash truck.

The girl's hand loops
Black strands of her
Waist-length hair up
To her pursed mouth,

As if to whisper to it;
Then comes the silent
Sweep of her pen, reveling
In secrets revealed at last.

Library Census

orange scent,
            i glance up
the edges of a slice being nibbled
                    and pages being parted,
                            lime after lime,
a blond in a lemon blouse
                ample and soft skin
            harvest basket, the musk of fragrance
    but a citrus face
                    behind the crate of stuffy books
                        peeling--
                                which sense is real?

Published in The Clockwise Cat

Rushing

Breathing toward death
                we recycle our past
            droning voices, destructive habits
repeatrepeatrepeatrepeatre

precious moments
                go
                    unmet   wasted
                                futures still born

stagnant shale
                stone shoal of Time
                                rushing......

The Revolution

They came ashore on the scythe of Cuba
On the small headed side of the island,
The rattled, saber-shaped isle of Batista,

To launch the new Marxist revolution
But got ambushed by Batista's trigger men
Who then retired to the decadent capital.

Che Guevara, slightly wounded, still
Managed to lead a rag-tag of the rebels
Away from the debacle into the heights.

For 9 days they lived on grass or raw corn,
Then macheted their destined way higher
Into the jungled Sierra Maestra mountains.

From those wild sides, these red rebels
Launched sniping skirmishes inland,
Down the coast, and toward rich Havana.

In one savage raid beneath a bony tree,
Che, the doctor, shot a short, swarthy Cuban,
(And later calmly noted in his journal

How the steel bullet had entered left
Of the man's brown eye), but quickly
Che, the victor, reached down to pull off

The dying soldier's glistening watch.
But the timepiece caught on the man's wrist bone,
And frowning, Che tugged forcefully on it.

"Yank, it off, boy," whispered the Cuban
As he grimaced in excruciating pain
And bled deep into the earth's blackness.

But ticking to the final judgment,
The revolting, revolving black hands
Of the coveted watch 'wouldn't' let go.

Previously published in Lucid Rhythms

The Slowness of Danger

He eased the old clunker
Of a Ford over to the tarred shoulder,
Where I stood thumbing west out of Bozeman;
I slung my worn rucksack
Into the back seat and plopped down
To my regret as I discerned too late
The plump driver was long-gone plastered,
Down with more than a 12-pack
All the way but not through the liver.

"I know I've had a few," he drawled,
"But I'm the most careful of drivers."
Then he slowed out onto the freeway,
Gas-pedaling up to 35 miles per hour,
While rushing vehicles swerved around
Past his slug of a sedan on the blacktop;
He gave new meaning and belied
The phrase about haste makes…

Published in Mad Swirl

My Ancestor's Tale

I suppose my surname, Wilcox, is ancestrally English,
But who'd want to be angled so proper and starched
With corruption stretched moldering round the world
Under the brilliant empired sun that never sets?

My dad says we're fightin' Scottish tee-totalers,
But who'd want to be such plaid, fork-tongued thieves
Who supplanted the Irish then sailed to the West,
To kill and greedily steal from the Redmen?

And my mom says we're devoutly half German,
But after the last two centuries who'd want Blood
And Iron skeletons in your closet of Bismark's
Lethal descended construction? Sink that!

When I was young, I wanted to turn native
Wear moccasins, be Dakota Sioux, Cheyenne
And put all the palefaces to backward flight;
I even dated Wa Ha Vet, a Cheyenne lass,

"Lady of the Clouds" and got my very own
Red name Ma Ga Vihet, "Curly White Spider"
With a dark tattoo to match hers on my left hand,
But she ran off with a Red brave and I returned

To the English fold; so what is the final take on
All this historic yak that obsesses our unkind?
The ancestral past lacks the eternal future,
Our true end—instead, seek to be humanly One.

Hardwood Tap Dancer

At the oak door
Your young golden retriever—
Who chewed through the metal
Water pipe and flooded your rental
Townhouse
Totally—
That infamous hound, now
Head wagging the air to tailed excess,
Greets me like his long lost master
In a bounding tap dance of 'appaws'
Clack, clack, clacking
Across your shiny hardwood floor
To a sliding dognail-scratched stop,
Frenzied movement and pointed-pup
Cold wet nosing;
With joy, he's the wonder
Jumper
Thumper
Prancer
Dancer
Of
Dog
Here
Ness.

Published in The Greensilk Journal

From below the line,
(Invisible and all)
Where I used to fish
For walleye and bass
In the northern lakes,
I still look up to Canada
As many a good soldier
And civilian look back
And up to Officer Montcalm
For his bravery and honor
In the Seven Years War.

From below the line
Where we killed Canadians
And Indians first by George
Washington's attack of
A diplomatic mission from
Up above; (our manifest destiny
Brutal ugly to a faulted fact);
Only last spring
Did the truth burst forth
In to my deluded mind,
Reeling from a surfeit
Of spurious print and
False American celluloid
Twisted and tangled down
Legends all falling wrong;

From below the line
I finally read academic
History and found Canada's
Montcalm opposed the killing
Of civilians and the disarmed,
For his northern honor
Was soldier to soldier,
Unlike us down under who

Paid 200 pounds
For a man's skinned head,
Half that for a woman's.

Up from below the line,
Yes, we cleansed the north,
Deporting Canadian civilians,
Enslaving thousands after
Killing the Field Marshall,
Who fought fairly; then
We fired Catholic churches and
Farms, but that's not terrorism
When we're so "right,"
Yeah right!

Yes, we're still below the line
Where we caught Chief Joseph
Trying to escape with civilians
To you, our northern foe;
Surely we're now ashamed for
All those our old Orwellian lies,
And I hear that Montcalm's
Bones have been reburied
And his honor restored;

But what frozen skeletons may
You Canadians have hiding
In your own secret closet
(We Southerners don't want
To be the only ones walking
The line)?

Published in The Centrifugal Eye

Redux

Like moose drool down from his jaw
Liquid drip of much after thought,
The human chews his abstract cud.

This brainy mammal with his huge
Mental jaw ruminates and masticates
Difficult philosophical concepts.

He chews and chews and chaws
Minding repeatedly, and pondering
Into his daily life for good or ill

The meta-conundrums, the ones
He can't stomach, the ethical gristle
Imponderable quandaries.

Like the massive moose of the glen,
Man Stands as king and all get out
In the damned lake he calls civilization;

Then walking into the tall trees, he
Rummages through the forest of ideas,
Philosophical redwoods towering above.

And he peers up searching the heights, but
Stands in the shadowed soggy morass,
The moral muddle of his shallow bog.

What festering future, or fertile destiny
Awaits this drooling race of man
Caught in the quagmire of himself?

Any St. Bernard dog, as Thoreau said,
Has more basic moral sense than
Most men who swallow gross sin whole.

Published in Words-Myth

Through Glass Darkly

Your maple eyes slow into me, a stork jar
Of turquoise tint, when I'm bent close to your face,
But alone of your presence I am empty;
Though I know you, it is through glass darkly—
Your vase of Indian rose shadowed from light
Partially shattered, lacerates my jarred lips;
But I would heal your broken tenderness and
Let the Son radiate through our glass colors
The surface round a violet hue of love.

Rim Ruin

red canyon
below the rim
a ruin hidden
beneath the arch of power
in the monolith of rock
a sheer cliff
standing before me--
and beyond—
breaking down
in the abyss of history

Orange-ugly carryall,
The hard Samsonite case
That doesn't really suit
His busy way in the garage;
He casts to the Goodwill.

Good riddance to that
More, yes less, blocking object
Cluttering his work space;
Now he can carry on.

But six months later his mate
Asks, Where's my suitcase?
I want to get out some fall
Blouses and warm skirts,
The ones I packed away
Last May; he had forgotten.

One more object obstructs
Their sight, blocks love's path;
Unwell, mutual vows remain
But the moonlight's soft beams
Eclipse, and the honey is so jarred
Empty no Indian summer warms
Their later years but unraveling trust,
Less and less until finally
Goodwill rejects his sorry self.

Stepping to William Wordsworth

I call to you
Out of the sandpaper scuff of my boots on the sidewalk
Where I come to its cantered edge,
I step down the curb side and walk across the width of the
coastal street,
Munching construction gravel under foot
And stare down into the aqua wash of the low lands of a
California
        Morning
Briskly brushed over raptap cottages and electric-blinking
monoliths,
And the worth of words to describe this wonder does not yet
appear—
Even you would have been wordless.

The Dog's Bite

The Tali-banned dog fighting
But America permits the dog-bite
Partying of religious Afghans
In the fanged gamble, their moneyed
Heroin poppies up, jagged blooms
Clawing the world market
Leech flowers blossoming deep, needle
In 'Vein' to others circusing the world round engulfed,
And the propped legislature votes
The blooded zenith
To execute apostates,
Ah well so sick
And punish blued wives who left
Hell! For several thousand bills, fighters
Can get out of jail free cards
So much jawing teeth
Dogging our 'warn' flag-budded tail.

Published in The Recusant

Before and After

Pictures past
In the verdant woods
Close to mountain cold streams
Our faces vibrant
Radiant and eager with zest
Remembrance of dreams planned
Hopes held close

Photos not taken now
Inside of cluttered rooms,
Distant demeanors
Filled with anxieties
Pensive looks and flat-out tired
Looking back to times lost
Despair strangles

Messed-Up News*

A USA porno tiger beauty torn
Pageant winner from Vegas Lost
Zoo mangled arm lines from
the tawdry news
downloaded photo smears
paw through the bars and
swipe the title
But the graphic 'gaud'
headline bodied
tittle—it's a
Keeper

Past News:
Tiger mauls keeper
Beauty queen loses
title because of vulgar pictures

Published in Crossing Rivers in Twilight

There in the urban lagoon
You are a sitting drunk
Gabbled to the bar
Waiting for the sotted-shot
To blast
Through your flapped brain
One more mallard
For the boat tender

Published in Word Riot

The Lady in the Garden

A picture-post-card date near the wide
Serpentine sway of the Susquehanna River
Meandering through Central Philly's park garden,
Towered over by leaning elms, while 3 long canoes
Swift by to the paddling of Ivy League collegians.

My Friendly girl, Grace, chestnut-caped round
In waist-length hair like a black ephod,
In her red chambray shirt and blue jeans,
Is an aspiring concert violinist but converses
Passionately of King's March to D.C. in 3 months.

I, the 'noble' drafted objector, work with lost-saken
Children confined to the gray mental ward
Disturbed by their absent parents' living,
But am still so youthfully focused and narrowed,
More concerned with my companion's
Figured shape than humanity's ship of state.

We sit cross-legged on the lush garden green,
Getting ready to eat our carefully bagged meal
Of 2 peanut butter and grape sandwiches
As we discuss the ravages of far-off Nam
And Bob Dylan's 'hard rained' croons.

But then I inhale this fuming putrid odor
Coming from behind; I twist my neck and see
About six feet away this bag of a lady in a filthy rag
Of a dress lunging slowly forward, hanging
Onto the ugly mesh of a shopping bag.
Her stench to high heaven wafts so rancid that
I pinch my nose tightly and turn away.

But lo and behold! my dear violinist rises
And welcomes the hag, "Hi Mam, will you join us
For a Sunday snack here in the sun?"

I am all upside down in my face as the homeless
One sprawls haggardly on the grass, her wretched,
Spotted shift wrinkling up her scraggly legs.
She reaches out a grubby hand, grabs one of our
Two sandwiches, and scoops half of it in her
Narrow jaws, chews open-mouthed and teethed.

I fume at this interloper, but then remember
The biblical story about the least of these
And finally join my musician's psalm
Under the swaying trees of compassioning.

Published in Oak Bend Review

Quit Flapping Your Gums

Quit flapping your gums
And your guns; we're not meant to be
Flappers of verbal excess
Or floggers of physical destruct,
Not broads or studs
But dispensers/wells/geysers
Of good/blessed/lighted tidings

Randy Rhody

where are you poet loss?
i remember back, as i kick sand here with my sandals
                              and listen to the ocean's
roar,
          you in your stretched blue sweater
                  hanging from your clothes-hanger frame
          as we discussed howling lines
                          and lyrics for the road.

are your corduroy pants legging it
                      down the streets of old town,
        or are you peering through the stacks at wisconsin's u.?

i fear you're no longer the shade of a wordworthed poet;
          sure your keatisian looks must've changed,
                    after confronting your martial rigid parent.

i miss your hungry face
                  which i fed in the nebraska cafeteria;
          you hardly ever raised a paw,
                        just sat there humbly
                              with eyes higher than
the clouds.

will i see you tomorrow?
                  a winner of the pulitzer,
          or are you breathless
                      from despair
          in some new york city slum
                        drastically successful in your second
try
in the kitchen stove,
                    no darlene, your dark angel, to shut the
gas in a poesque,
              yet again, rescue.

whatever, wherever-
            i'd like you to know i'm caught too in the muse
of sphere's so effusive
        that if I finish my dreamed novel of America's night,
                       i'll drink from the
fountain for you.

A Question of Human Real Estate

Past the green vines fecund with grapes
On the sturdy side of the black couple's home
Where a faded porch swing gentles in its arc;

Then slowly driving over the ship-high bridge--
Vast bay vistas stretch widening our eyes,
Mounting hills and inlets of the Pacific,

Down to the fuming refineries of Richmond,
Past storefronts clapboarded, vacant facades
That scrawl down the hunched gray streets

To the brazed corner below the liquored light
Where by the hydrant, 3 listing black youth slump
Against the news—narrow, vacant-slothed eyes.

Published in Word Catalyst Magazine

The Day of Dying

Living on the lush island
In that new time of '68
Near Washington's Crossing
Close to New Hope, Pennsylvania
Where William penned a new state,
Founded His Holy Experiment
Transforming human government
Until the Seven Years War
And its white land lust
Scalped away the Ocean of Light—
Each native woman's head
Selling for 100 British pounds--
So the Friends resigned in mass
From the Legislature unwilling
To arm White raging muskets.

But here I live 210 years later
After crossing the stream at the ford,
Like I do each morning and even,
Showering with a cold bucket
Of water behind a blanket
Draped over my open
Van doors, living in
My Chevy Greenbriar
I have christened
The Mystical Hippopotamus,
Because my right-wing landlord
Kicked me out for
My anti-Nam sign
On the van's rear..

Comes the humid night
Of the presidential primaries
When I sit on the edge
In the driver's seat
Going no where fast,

Gripping the red wheel
Listening to the sad turns
When Eugene McCarthy
Falls down to tragic defeat
Like a cherry tree before it time,
And the long shadow of 50ish
Joseph, his Hydian twin
The 'right' but wrong
Batters the American dream,
Assaulting 'this land is yours'
With more killing of natives,
This time of the Viet unkind;
The dream of Paine loses to the
Nightswine mudded wrong;
Eugene's vision poked out.

On this night, I curse the darkness
But when I try to start my engine
The key only rotates the starter
For my battery has died
From listening to the death
Of my generation's ideals
And lost new hopes
Another crossing indeed
But not of the revolutionary kind.
William 'penns' the obituary,
The dying of Martin's
Lighted Dream.

Published in The Clockwise Cat

Moments flash
Like falling meteors burning out
Precious glories
While I pine for the remote quasar
Whose light taunts me
One who ceased to burn
A millennial ago
Light years away

Leaf

I turn
A hard crinkled leaf
Wind-blowing across the concrete
Scraping staccato
What if I step on it?

No More Down Under

I'm not whistling down "Dixie"
When I say blokes have overtaken
The far Northwest's whitened trails.
At Whistler's mother of all resorts,
The ski-bummed heaven fairly roo-
Hops with Aussies at every waterhole,
Or iced, some other snow job party?
An avalanche of Down Unders
Riding the banks over cliff and dale;

Former lonely mining land now
Shiver-me-timbers clear cut,
The stumps low, cropped so down
Outback of the high-rise rentals;
Rooms fill on partying BC Day.
What's that? I ask at a busy 7-11
In Vancouver. Who knows? the clerk says.

And he hands me a large toonie;
Maybe it means Beyond Canada?
Below Cambera (via Antarctica)?
Where no one is a red maple leafer
Except the famed mounted police
In their dark SUV's and the flags
Leafing the sky before the snow.

But what a walkabout! Over
Thousands of miles of watery blue,
How'd you do it, sharked mates?
At the next store full of the southern drawl,
I say, I bet you're an Aussie
But the chap glances up with disdain;
No way, I'm a Kiwi!

Dove of an Eagle

Cesar Chavez
Living martyr very un-Roman
Humble eagle of the San Joaquin
Rises over green fields and rich earth
A skyward move for impoverished workers
Son of the hungry and downtrodden
Short , stocky, swarthy
Commanding words of power to arise
Migrating, marching, striking, fasting
The Olive Branch of the UFW

Of the Memory

From the orange-treed, brown San Joaquin valley
In the small California town of Orland
To the green rolling hills of alfalfa and corn
Outside of Table Rock near shallow Clear Creek
Where the farm boy Don grew up thin and tall,

To the tall-oaked streets and little houses
In the small Nebraska town of Pawnee
To the blue-gray home, separate brown garage
And verdant green garden on the edge
Where the town girl Elma rose to the call;

Through the troubled waters of violent strife in
The Pacific aboard the cruiser Salt Lake
Radioing Morse Code from ship to ship
A sailor winning the Day against tyranny,

Through the tragic waters of loss on the
Busy town street where the crashing Ford passed
Mourning her young brother, praying and seeking,
A store clerk working her way against tragedy;

Coming together on a cool Thursday night
At the red-bricked Baptist church in the middle
Of town, but then displaced by the war's horror,
Finally wedding in the new peace face to face;

Going, going, always going, he and she
Are the Ever-Ready couple reaching out in
Gifts to their loved ones and ministering
To others at the many places they graced.

Going still at this elderly age, sharing
Their loving kindness and diligent work
They grow up in giving blessed Heaven anew,
Their time of sharing, dining, and 60th embrace.

Lost?

Lost?
Seek the moral compass
Round the world ringed that
Bleeds directed compass-ion;
Don't pass by on the other side;
Be passionate
And encompass
Love's Sphere
Found.

My dream fades
A gardened collage rapidly
Receding, swallowed
By the hard angles of the night
And then the glare of the waking

At a Slow Run

Death comes at a slow run
Down the rotted streets
Life's ruts
Old age clocks my days
In a time duel
Frantic in the anxious crawl
I'm misplaced
Grasping for the
Ruby clasp of felled beauty
Used coins of time vanish
After the upward toss
The magician's trick
Death comes at a slow run

Underneath the dogged sun
      a woolly mop-headed romantic
            floundered in the bogs of despair,
     holding his heart and brain in hand
          pondering which to throw
            or how to keep both.

The Fall Estate Sale

Worrying about their upcoming fall trip,
A 60th-anniversary wedded cruise to Alaska,
My 79-year-old mother joked about air disaster;
Said, "When the plane goes down, me and father
Will go up." I pause and wonder at the heavenly quip.

Hours falling-star pass me as I slowly tree-ring
My way through the daily grind to my own demise.
Hopefully the atheists of the press muse wrongly.
And when our limbs become stark like great oaks,
We will later leave anew in the bud of old falling up.
Such feathered hope wisps above the great Death Valley
Of modern, fallen knowledge, rising in each March breeze.

Why am I chewing such ugly gristle so early in the autumn
With three-quarters of a beef cow still frozen stiff in our
freezer?
As I move stack after stack of seasoned books from the
summer
Of my years, trying to gain organization in my composted
house--
No longer triple booking the shelves--I can already hear the
Canadian
Winds yet to blow down through the Dakotas over my
parents'
And ancestors' graves where the Nebraska leavings aren't
raked.

In the small pioneer village of yester-seasoned with grace
soon
Salted with cold granules that turn to slush in a brief Indian
season,
I keep postponing the inevitable, the fallen estate sale of
Our Egyptian remains before the stark blizzards come
And bury us under like the white sand of Los Alamos.

Confused Poet

ever hear
of the absent-minded poet
who plunged his teeth
and flossed the toilet?

Vicki

sunburned and peeling
with two braids and indian bead
        read the look of my eyes
                yours are green

depressed and feeling
        with worn jeans and painted flower
                tower above your sadness
                        don't give up

abused and needing
with small feet and rounded figure
        sure you are pretty
                i dig you

confused and being
with personality and shadow eyes
        try and care for others
                for you are loved

The Tick

politics, many ticks sucking
the life out of minding relationships
tics of nerves lost
and ticking to twelve

the slip and the rats' race

the sharking attitudes of
swamp tailgating
political gators

a still life of falling clocks timed

aren't you tickled?

vote for...

Twisted Cider

sui cider
tamil tigers
those humans so grueling
for sri lankan land,
flesh and bone 'cannon-bals'
devouring with teched nashing

Our Stripes

swirl, grasp, hoard,
blood drums silently
            red

god, war, dam-nation,
flag grins skeleton
            white

tech, demise, death
music moans noted
            blue

Rounding the Wheel

Rotating human mill wheel
Slosh, cascade, drain, spill
Chained ever backward
Hade-ed below
To the descending
Downward dark buckets,

Thoughtless lemmings
Spilling awareness,
Consciousness punished
Dragged ever under
Drowning in the
River Styxian whirl
Submerged, then gasp
Pulled up awake,

Another 'roted' day
Round and round
And down-looping
Repeating failure,
Pinwheeling sin
Endlessly

The dealing,
Recycling our past roll
Over and over and over
Under the Sisyphean
Wheelering

Unless
We center
Our selves
To the
Hub

Jagged cordage, tangled and jumbled
The junk of modern confusion
Bundled nerves twisted and tossed
Overboard
Anchorless
In this body's 'sea'
No rime or mariner
In this

Restless wave
The curve and break;

To find a touchstone
On the eternal shore
To be a warm Buddha in the sun

The Tightrope

The tightrope miracle
To be present in the moment
Between birth and death
Rather than skyrocketing futures
Or dead-bogged pasts
More difficult than the highest trapeze
The eternal balance
Of the
Moment

Dirge in the Night

I

During the dark time,
No winged dream
Or blinded vision
But many an entreaty
Of suffering supplication,
Yet
Out of the swollen belly of Sheol
Come the horded onslaught
Of night's cavalry
Thundering boldly forth,
Black hooves of clodded loss.

II

Episodic night-criers
Ring their clarion warnings
Iron bells of ever told
(Ask not for whom),
Dark symbolic forebodings
None is right, none is left
Through the streets of our mind
In this philosophical slum,
Map-less and encompassed
In darkened loss.

III

Hanging from the talking wires
Hope abandoned, forsaken
A worn 'souled' shoe deserted
Above the crowded road of pavement
Winding in the buffeting wind of chance,
Swinging, strung up by historical
High-wire acts
Between the telephone crosses.

IV

To the Forsaken One,
Be my vision, we cry,
Phrasing our deepest needs
Like verbal tourniquets,
The bleeding endlessly red
Calvary still
While we parse our verbs
Unreachable goals
Hell to pay,
But irised
To the
Light.

Published in Danse Macabre

The Need

Not vague generalities
So forever downdated,
Spit from mouth to ear
Dribbled abstraction--
Wipe away that spittle.

We need triggers of hope,
Hot particulars
Heating pockets for the soul,
Warm possibilities
Melting on the tongue,
Soothing the drum
Of our reality.

Wa-ha-vet

no letter;
    made a phone call

what is wrong;
    don't care at all

i don't know,
    blank like a wall

bye I said;
    eyes down fall

many joys;
    sadly recall

day is gone
    and now nightfall

The Lifeline

I squinted and tried to see
The far shore cliff
High and lifted up
Above the churning
River rapiding to the falls
Where not so long ago
The heavy rope life-lined,
That used to stretch up
Taut with expectancy
Across the chasm
To the sunned ridge
Beyond the plummet
To the dark canyon below;

But now the thick cable lays
Useless on the slated granite
And dangles hopelessly
Down into the noisy torrent;
Unconnected far above
The unreachable heights dim
In the distant rainbowed mist.

Earlier when the ripping disconnect
Came, the strong cable snapped
In the middle and plummeted
Down, whipping into the river
Snaking into the swirling depths
Of the current's torrent
And unrelenting force.

I pulled at the wet cordage
And dragged the rope
Slowly up from the swiftly
Moving caldron of froth
Of the deluged river below.
I heaved with both hands and

My arm muscles bulged as
I pulled the former lifeline in
And ached as I wound the cable,
Soaked and icy cold
Around the dull wheel housing
Before me grounded
Here.

I circled and circled the wheel
Until all of the thick rope
Rounded going nowhere
Above the gross torrent;
Then came the frayed middle end

Where the stretched 'hope' had
From the traversing weight
Of so many tons of expecteds
The heavy-weighted dreams
Of my limitless youth.

The One in Need

He drove us to drink
In his ceaseless quest
To achieve respect.

Look out here comes
The driver of drunks,
Still looking for renown

But should he ever
Get the famed overhang
All bottle up and capped

The downside of this
Is that he will ever
Be crowded alone.

The Ultimatum

In my every moment's thought
And my daily eventual, each second's act
Is finite's harsh ultimatum
The living 'dun' comes due
Sooner than soon than yesterday, boxed
And past acted wrongs
Wrap your still carcass
Shrouding lost potential
Historical decay reigns
Never change
The coin of past decisions
Bankruptures
And there is no operation
To repair
A mental hernia
Nor the 'souled' one
Only love's ultimate grace
From above/within truth
Will
Kill
Our premature
Burial

Fall Eyes

Fall eyes spoke
        more than surface words could say,
    but I played hide
      and seek behind my beliefs,
        afraid of
        fall
        ing

      but such plastic piety

              denies
authenticity.

Then what do I now?
      Though
       I inked your offered hand
    with my street and town
      your
        England letters have
never
come,
   and music which I wouldn't hear

             is not

silent in me now.

Published in Gambit

Yosemite
Half Dome
Granite monolith eoned in time
Glaciated but not destroyed
Majestic Time Lord
Unaware of the Eternal
Ever mattered

daniel
half done
fragile being decaded in years
ruined and soon inert
temporary time slave
conscious of the Ultimate
soon matterless

why?

Daniel Wilcox earned his degree in Creative Writing from Cal State University, Long Beach. A former activist, teacher, and wanderer--from Montana to the Middle East-- he casts his lines out upon the world's turbulent waters and wide shores in *Counterexample Poetics, Moria, The Centrifugal Eye, Tipton Poetry Journal, Lunarosity, Wild Violet, Oak Bend Review, The Writer's Eye, Lucid Rhythms,The Recusant*, etc. A short story, "The Faces of Stone" based on his time in the Middle East, appeared in both *The Danforth Review* and *Danse Macabre*. Daniel has completed a speculative novel *The Feeling of the Earth* and is working on another poetry collection, *Psalms, Yawps, and Howls*. He lives with his mysterious wife on the central coast of California.

Website: http://seaquaker.com

Printed in the United States
221310BV00001B/5/P